The Rockwool Foundation Research Unit

Study Paper No. 76

Is Leadership in the Eye of the Beholder?

A Study of Intended and Perceived Leadership Strategies and Organizational Performance

Christian Bøtcher Jacobsen and
Lotte Bøgh Andersen

University Press of Southern Denmark

Odense 2014

Is Leadership in the Eye of the Beholder?

A Study of Intended and Perceived Leadership Strategies and Organizational Performance

Study Paper No. 76

Published by:
© The Rockwool Foundation Research Unit

Address:
The Rockwool Foundation Research Unit
Soelvgade 10, 2.tv.
DK-1307 Copenhagen K

Telephone	+45 33 34 48 00
E-mail	forskningsenheden@rff.dk
web site:	www.en.rff.dk

ISBN 978-87-93119-18-5
ISSN 0908-3979

August 2014

ABSTRACT

The HRM literature argues that intended leadership practices can be perceived entirely different by employees, and that perceived practices are more likely to be related to performance than intended practices, because perceived practices are closer related with motivation and commitment. A strong tradition in the leadership literature distinguishes between transformational and transactional leadership strategies and expects both types of leadership to be related to performance. This literature often defines leadership by how it is intended by leaders, but typically measures leadership as it is perceived by employees. Using a sample of 1,621 teachers and 79 Danish high schools, we find that intended and perceived transformational and transactional leadership strategies are only weakly correlated, and that only perceived strategies (both transformational and transactional) are significantly related to objectively measured school performance. The results point to the importance of separating between intended and perceived practices and that leaders should pay attention towards how their practices are perceived.

INTRODUCTION

Most studies of leadership take the employees' perception of the leadership behavior as the point of departure, but it remains unclear how the leaders' own perception of their leadership strategy matters. This is an important question, because it touches upon how we should study leadership, and what perceived leadership is. It is also important knowledge for leaders, because they need to know whether their intended leadership behavior will have an effect through their employees' perceptions of this leadership. This paper sets out to study the relationship intended leadership (reported by leaders), perceived leadership (reported by employees) and organizational performance in public organizations (according to register data).

We use the classical leadership distinction between transformational and transactional leaders. Whereas transformational leaders stimulate their employees and change their beliefs, assumptions, and behaviors by appealing to the importance of collective or organizational outcomes, transactional leaders instead direct their attention at the employees' self-interest by offering rewards or threatening with sanctions (Moynihan, Pandey, & Wright, 2012). Existing studies have shown the relevance of the transformational-transactional distinction in the public sector (Bellé, 2013; Moynihan et al., 2012; Oberfield, 2012; Van Wart, 2013), but no studies have, to our knowledge, combined information about leadership strategy from both leaders and employees with performance data from public organizations. A few studies have studied leadership and performance using either subjectively measured performance data (Oberfield, 2012; Park & Rainey, 2008; Trottier, Van Wart, & Wang, 2008) or focusing on relatively narrow aspects of objectively performance due to experimental designs (Bellé, 2013; Dvir, Eden, Avolio, & Shamir, 2002). In addition to this paper's focus on intended versus perceived leadership, we contribute by supplementing those studies with knowledge about the leadership-performance relationship for broader, long term performance measures in a real life setting. The overall research question is: *What is the relationship between leaders' assessment of their own leadership strategies and their employees' perceptions of these leadership strategies, and how do these different assessments of leadership relate to organizational performance?*

We investigate this question empirically in the area of upper secondary education in Denmark. This is a well-suited area, because the employees refer to one leader in clearly hierarchical organizations, and there is variation in transactional and transformational leadership strategies and in school performance. We have highly reliable performance data in the form of register data on student grades (school effects controlled for a number of social demographic variables). Furthermore, we have gathered survey data from around 80 school leaders (principals) and 2,300 employees (teachers). This allows us to perform analyses of 1) the relationship between the leaders' assessment of their own leadership and employees' perceptions of these leadership strategies, and 2) study the relationship between these perceptions and organizational performance controlled for a number of variables, which could potentially influence the grade levels. The study can therefore offer a unique contribution to our knowledge about what leadership in the public sector is, and what its effects are on organizational performance.

THEORETICAL FRAMEWORK

Intended and perceived leadership behaviors

Typically, leadership is theoretically described as it is intended by leaders (Avolio, Bass, & Jung, 1999; Bass & Riggio, 2006), but on the measurement side, almost all studies measure leadership as it is perceived by employees (Avolio, Reichard, Hannah, Walumbwa, & Chan, 2009; Bass & Riggio, 2006). The HRM literature has, however, argued that intended and perceived practices can be entirely different. Intended practices are those "that the firm's decision makers believe will effectively elicit the employee responses desired" (Wright & Nishii, 2007: 9). However, intended practices will, due to implementation challenges, not necessarily transform into actual practices, and actual practices will be "perceived and interpreted subjectively by each employee" (Paauwe & Boselie, 2005; Wright & Nishii, 2007). Separating intended and perceived practices has important consequences for conceptualization as well as measurement of leadership practices, because "there is likely to be a disconnect between intended HR practices as reported by managers and the effect of actual HR practices that is at least partially explained by differential meanings imposed on those practices by employees" (Nishii, Lepak, & Schneider, 2008: 528). Furthermore, according to the HRM literature perceived practices are much more likely to be related to organizational performance than intended practices, because perceived practices are related to employee motivation and commitment and employee responses to practices, and these aspects are often decisive for the performance effects of a given leadership practice (Wright & Nishii, 2007). Figure 1 illustrates how intended practices can affect actual practices which again can affect perceived practices. According to Wright and Nishii (2007), employee reactions and ultimately performance depend on these perceived practices rather than directly on intended or actual practices.

Figure 1. Process model of leadership practices*

* Based on Wright & Nishii, 2007

The ambition of much leadership literature is to study the effects of *actual* leadership practices, but this concept is very difficult to measure by other methods than observation (which can be problematic, because leaders and employees might act differently if they are observed). The practical solution is usually to study perceived leadership practices (collected in employee surveys). In addition to the difficulty of measuring actual leadership practices, it is also reasons to expect that perceived practices can be even more relevant. We would only expect leadership to be effective if it is actually perceived by the individuals, and there can also be differences in how for example the organizational vision is clarified and motivated individually. The strong tradition for measuring leadership strategy among employees might therefore be very reasonable. There is, however, still very relevant to actually investigate the relationship between intended practices and perceived practices. Leaders' perceptions of their own leadership strategy will reflect their intentions, and it is interesting analyze how this corresponds to the employees' perceptions, because both leaders and researchers need to know the degree to which intentions are actually translated to leadership perceived by employees. To our knowledge, only one other study, which was carried out in the private sector, analyze this question, and their results suggest significant discrepancies (Tekleab, Sims, Yun, Tesluk, & Cox, 2008). To our knowledge, no public sector study uses a similar approach. There are (at least) to ways to evaluate the usefulness of studying intended and perceived leadership: We can look at the association between the two concepts (if the correlation is very high, both might be fruitful, and it may not matter much how we study leadership), and we can analyze the relationship between leadership and performance, using different leadership concepts and then comparing the associations. In public organizations, performance can be defined as achievement of the objectives formulated by elected politicians. Below, we will conceptualize leadership in terms of different leadership strategies and discuss how we specifically expect these leadership strategies to be associated to performance. In other words, the next sections will explicate the following general expectations:

H1: Employee perceptions of leadership behavior and leader intended leadership behavior are positively associated, but not so strongly correlated that the concepts can be said to capture the same phenomenon.

H2: Employee perceptions of leadership behavior rather than leader intended leadership behavior are related with organizational performance.

Transformational and transactional leadership

We do, as mentioned, use the concepts transactional and transformational leadership in our conceptualization. These concepts were first introduced by Burns (1978) to capture differences between political leaders, but following Bass' (Bass, 1985) theoretical improvements of the theory, focus shifted towards the private sector. However, a number of recent studies have demonstrated the relevance of these two leadership strategies in public organizations (Bellé, 2013; Moynihan et al., 2012; Oberfield, 2012; Park & Rainey, 2008; Trottier et al., 2008; Wright, Moynihan, & Pandey, 2009). Following Bass, transactional leaders "lead through social exchange", whereas transformational leaders "stimulate and inspire followers to both achieve extraordinary outcomes and, in the process, develop their own leadership capacity" (Bass & Riggio, 2006: 3). According to Bass, transformational leadership consists of four dimensions. Idealized influence is when the leader serves as a role model, and when employees ascribe ideal attributes to their leader. Inspirational motivation involves articulating an appealing and inspiring vision of the future and motivating, inspiring, and committing employees to pursue it. Intellectual stimulation is when leaders encourage employees to be innovative and creative. Finally, individual consideration is the special attention to the individual needs of employees through mentoring, coaching etc. Transactional leadership consists of three dimensions. Contingent reward is the assignment or obtainment of employee agreement on goals with rewards for satisfactory results. Active management-by-exception is monitoring of deviances from standards, mistakes and errors, and passive management-by-exception is passively waiting for deviances from standards, mistakes and errors (Bass & Riggio, 2006: 6-8).

Critics of Bass' model of leadership have pointed to a number of issues concerning both concepts, mechanisms and measurement of leadership (Van Knippenberg & Sitkin, 2013). Particularly a clear definition of transformational leadership is missing, so it can be assessed what the boundaries of the concepts are, and "there is no statement of what conceptually unites the different elements and identifies or distinguishes them as being charismatic–transformational leadership" (Ibid.: 10). The same critics have pointed to the visionary element of transformational as the core of Bass' concept of transformational leadership (Ibid.: 46). Visionary leadership can be defined as "the verbal communication of an image of a future for a collective with the intention to persuade others to contribute to the realization of that future". We agree that the leadership literature suffers from unclear and potentially overlapping concepts, and that the most promising solution is to focus on the central aspect of articulating a clear and inspiring vision in order to induce extraordinary performance. We therefore see transformational leadership as "behaviors intended to develop, share, and sustain a vision in order to facilitate that employees transcend their own self-interest and achieve organization goals". In contrast, transactional leadership is "the use of contingent rewards and sanctions intended to facilitate that employees' self-interest makes them achieve organization goals". While it is clear that active and passive management-by-exception is aimed at employee self-interest, rewards in the public sector might be used more as a token or an appreciation of employees' efforts and commitments to organizational goals (Andersen & Pallesen, 2008). To make sure that we can differentiate between the leadership strategies, we focus on management-by-exception in our conceptualization of transactional leadership in this paper. We therefore test the following implications of hypothesis 1:

H1a: Employees' perceptions of their leader's level of transactional leadership (conceptualized as management-by-exception) and their leader's perceptions of his/her own (intended) level of this leadership strategy are positively associated, but not so strongly correlated that the concepts can be said to capture the same phenomenon.

H1b: Employees' perceptions of their leader's level of transformational leadership and their leader's perceptions of his/her own (intended) level of this leadership strategy are positively associated, but not so strongly correlated that the concepts can be said to capture the same phenomenon.

Performance and the investigated leadership strategies

In relation to our second hypothesis (expecting that employee perceptions of leadership behavior rather than leader intended leadership behavior are related with organizational performance), it is relevant to discuss how and why we expect our investigated leadership strategies (transformational and transactional leadership) to affect performance. In our conceptualization, transactional leadership is based on the use of sanctions of pecuniary and non-pecuniary nature related to the employees' performance (Bass 1985;

Antonakis et al. 2003; Avolio 2004). If transactional leaders punish employees when their work effort and results are unsatisfactory, this disciplining will make it costly for the employees to deviate from the leaders' directions. If employees shirk or sabotage, they risk to loose privileges and ultimately be fired. If the employees are (also) extrinsically motivated, transactional leadership strategies are expected to have positive effects on performance. Existing studies have found transactional leadership strategies to be somewhat effective towards both employee outcomes such as job satisfaction and motivation as well as on perceived quality (Oberfield, 2012; Park & Rainey, 2008). The implication of hypothesis 2 in relation to this leadership strategy is therefore:

H2a: Employee perception of transactional leadership (conceptualized as management-by-exception) rather than the leader's intended level of this leadership strategy is positively associated with organizational performance.

Existing research has consistently found that transformational leadership is positively associated with employee performance both generally (Avolio et al., 2009; Bass & Riggio, 2006; Bernard M. Bass, 1999; Lowe, Kroeck, & Sivasubramaniam, 1996) and in the public sector (Bellé, 2013; Dvir et al., 2002; Trottier et al., 2008; Wofford, Whittington, & Goodwin, 2001). Transformational leadership is expected to clarify organizational goals and increase the congruence between organizational and employee values and thereby positively affect motivation (Bass & Riggio, 2006; Paarlberg & Lavigna, 2010; Ritz, 2009). With the aim of directing and inspiring individual effort, transformational leaders try to transform (and motivate) their followers by raising their awareness of the importance of organizational values. This leadership strategy does, in other words, aim at affecting performance indirectly through the employees' motivation and values. We expect transformational leadership to be effective, because it "augments transactional leadership to achieve higher levels of subordinate performance with the primary difference residing in the process by which the leader motivates subordinates and in the types of goals set" (Lowe et al., 1996), and the implication of hypothesis 2 for this leadership strategy is therefore:

H2b: Employee perception of transformational leadership rather than the leader's intended level of this leadership strategy is positively associated with organizational performance.

Transformational leadership has sometimes been described as superior leadership (Seltzer & Bass, 1990), but there has been an increasing recognition, that transactional aspects are inherent to much of organizational functioning, such as pay structures, career paths, and performance management (Van Wart, 2013). Waldman et al. (1990) argue that the best leadership is both transformational and transactional, because transformational behaviors reinforce the positive effect of contingent reward behaviors and lead to greater levels of subordinate effort and performance. The existing few studies of the combined effect of the leadership strategies (Rowold 2011; Hargis et al. 2011; O'Shea et al. 2009; Bass et al. 2003) also suggest that combined transactional/transformational leadership leads to even higher performance than any of the leadership strategies separately. Thus, whereas transformational and transactional leadership strategies were originally posited as contrasts (Burns 1978), they do not necessarily conflict (Waldman et al. 1990), and we therefore see the two leadership strategies as different continua. Thus, we argue that both leadership strategies can be effective simultaneously.

RESEARCH DESIGN AND METHODS

Studying Danish upper secondary schools

This study uses Danish upper secondary schools (publicly owned and funded) to test the hypotheses, because this area provides at least four advantages. First, we can relatively easily link employees (teachers) with their leader (the school principal), since the principals is responsible for personnel management for all teachers at a given school. Second, Danish upper secondary schools are very similar, because they produce more or less identical services, and this allows us to study a highly comparable performance outcome, school effects, and also to keep a number of potentially confounding variables constant. Third, a recent reform in this area has allowed the principals much more power and autonomy, which provides them better opportunities to actively exert their leadership. Fourth and finally, simultaneously gathered survey data is available for both leaders (school principals) and employees (teachers).

In the Danish school system, the first ten years of basic schooling (*grundskole*) are mandatory (grades 0 through 9), and after graduation students are obliged to continue their education in either a vocational school or a high school. This study focuses on high schools, which provide nationally regulated, tuition-free, general education to more than half of the Danish youth (around 65.000 students in 2010 according to The Ministry of Children and Education, 2010). The schools fall into three categories: 1) The General Upper Secondary Education Program (Stx), 2) The Higher Commercial Examination Program (Hhx), and 3) The Higher Technical Examination Program (Htx). Stx offers a range of subjects in the fields of the natural and social sciences as well as humanities, Hhx focuses on business and economic disciplines in combination with general subjects, and Htx focuses on technological and scientific subjects in combination with general subjects (Hvidman & Sivertsen, 2013). Thus, the focus varies slightly between schools, but they share the common objective of ensuring students general education, knowledge, and competences and they all qualify for access to higher education.

All three school types have relatively high levels autonomy and are self-governing with their own supervisory boards and financed through activity-based budgeting (based on the number of students enrolled and passing exams). Thus, school principals in all three school types are in relatively strong formal positions to exert their leadership. Internally, the schools all have a relatively flat structure with short distance from principal to the teachers. Thus, principals have personnel management responsibility for the teachers, and most of them interact with the teachers on a daily basis. Although middle management probably takes up more resources than earlier, the tasks of middle managers are mainly administrative, whereas personnel management primarily remains with the principals. On this background there is good reason to expect that principals can exert influence on school performance through the teachers.

Methods of analysis

To study the correlation between employees' and leaders' perceptions of the leadership strategies, we use bivariate correlations, because we want to find out whether the two concepts capture the same empirical phenomenon. We could have controlled for employees characteristics (such as age and gender), but we find that it is more relevant to see whether the "raw scores" are similar. If employee and leaders assessments are similar only after control for socio-demographic factors, it still suggests that it is important for future research to choose between them. Only if the bivariate correlation is very high, this decision becomes inconsequential. We look at both individual employee perceptions in relation to their leader's perception and on the aggregated employee perception in a given organization in relation to the perception of the leader of this organization. We use Pearson's r> 0.8 as criterion for evaluate whether the concepts can be said to measure the same phenomenon. This choice balances two conflicting considerations: While a value gives more certainty that the concepts can be said to reflect the same, there is also measurement errors in both measures. Pearson's r = 0.8 means that one concept explains 64 % of the variation in the other concept. To study the association between the two leadership strategies and organizational performance, we use OLS regressions with schools as units of analyses. If we had had data on individual performance, we could also have performed a multilevel analysis, but it is not meaningful, given that we only have information about the dependent variable on the organizational level. In the OLS regressions, we control for a number of school level characteristics, which may be associate both leadership and school performance. Specifically, we control for the leader's gender, age, and tenure in the current position (as suggested in Eagly & Johnson, 1990; Meier, O'Toole, & Goerdel, 2006). We also control for school size (number of teachers, given that performance via for example organizational commitment can negatively related to organization size and also matter for leadership strategy) and for mean teacher age and tenure, because teacher experience may be associated with better performance. Gender composition (share of women among the teachers) is also included due to the potential gender effects on both leadership and performance (Eagly & Johnson, 1990).

Data

We have approached all 144 STX schools in Denmark with an invitation to participate in two parallel surveys directed at the managerial level and the employee level respectively. In October 2012 we sent a letter to the schools, where we requested contact information for principals, middle managers and teachers. Most schools sent us the information, and for most of the remaining schools, we were able to gather information from their websites. Nine schools were left out of the investigation either because they actively refused to participate, or because we could not obtain contact information. In late November, we sent web-based questionnaires to 135 principals and 8,600 teachers, and throughout December we sent four reminders to those, who had not yet responded. When the survey was closed on December 21st, 95 principals and 3,200 teachers had completed the survey (response rates 60.3 percent and 34.1 percent respectively). 79 principal responses were complete, and we use these and the 1,621 teachers at these schools in the analyses below.

Measures

The performance measure applied here is school effects. We have obtained exam mark information from highly reliable registers. Statistics Denmark thus collects data on all Danish high school students' exam marks. "The observed grade level" is the school means of all externally graded written exams. "The expected grade level" is then calculated based on social demographic variables at the school level (gender, birth year, parents' education level, parents' income (in DKK), parents' employment, parents' age and ethnicity). The school effect is then calculated as the expected grade level subtracted from the observed grade level, resulting in positive school effects, if observed grade levels are higher than expected and vice versa. In other words, the performance measure (school effect) is positive if student exam marks are higher than should be expected based on the students' background and negative if student exam marks are lower than should be expected.

All other variables in the study are measured in multiple survey items from the surveys to employees (teachers) and leaders (school principals). We have coupled employee and leader responses into the same dataset. The wording of some of the items varies slightly to fit with the relevant type of respondent. For leadership strategy, the questions for example open with either 'As a leader I...' or 'My leader...'. All items have been taken from previously validated and commonly used measures. We have translated all items to English and back again to validate the content of the items. Before the actual survey, we ran a pilot study to 150 employees and one leader, which resulted in adjustments of the surveys. Primarily, the survey was shortened, but the wording of some items was also changed. Transformative leadership and transactional leadership are measured among both employees and leaders. Transformational leadership is measured with items taken from Podsakoff et al. (1993), Trottier et al. (2008), and Wright et al. (2012), and the items measuring transactional leadership strategy were taken from Trottier et al. (2008) and Den Hartog et al. (1997). Among both employees and leaders, we find loadings round 0.6 for management-by-exception. For transformational leadership, the loadings were around 0.80 for employees and 0.7 for leaders (except one item among leaders). We will return to this point in the discussion section. We include a number of control variables, including age, gender, and experience of both employees and leader, which were all gathered in the survey, and also we control for the number of employees, which comes from our lists of respondents, which cover all teachers at each school. Table 1 shows the summary statistics of all variables.

Table 1: Sample characteristics ($n_{leaders}$ = 79, $n_{employees}$ = 1.621)

	M	SD	Min	Max
Organizational level				
School effect	-0.002	0.222	-.0470	0.615
Transformational leadership	80.1	12.3	31.25	100
Transactional leadership (mbe)	40.1	21.1	0	75
Leader age	57.8	6.1	42	69
Leader gender (female = 1)	0.22	0.41	0	1
Leader's tenure (years, current school)	11.5	7.1	1	31
School size (no. of teachers)	90.2	35.7	18	164
Employee level				
Transformational leadership	50.4	24.9	0	100
Transactional leadership (mbe)	32.9	22.9	0	100
Age	45.4	11.1	24	71
Gender (female = 1)	0.52	0.50	0	1
Tenure (years, current school)	11.4	10.8	0	46

RESULTS

The results section is divided into two sections. We first look at the leaders' intended leadership and the employees' perceptions of the leaders' leadership to see how they are related. This is followed by an analysis of the associations between the leadership strategies (intended and/or perceived) and organizational performance.

Table 2: Intended and perceived leadership strategies

	M	SD	Min	Max
Transformational leadership				
Intended (leaders' assessment)	80.1	12.3	31.25	100
Perceived (employees' assessment)	50.4	24.9	0	100
Transactional leadership (management-by-exception)				
Intended (leaders' assessment)	40.1	21.1	0	75
Perceived (employees' assessment)	32.9	22.9	0	100

Table 2 reveals that there is substantial discrepancy between intended and perceived leadership behaviors, particularly in relation to transformational leadership. Whereas the leaders on average rate their own transformational leadership to be 80.1 on a 0-100 scale, the employees only perceive it to be 50.4. A correlation analysis (table 2) shows that the Pearson's r between the individual employee's perception of transformational leadership and the leader's intended transformational leadership is only 0.038 (not significant at the 0.05 level). For aggregated employee perception of transformational leadership, the correlation between the leader's own assessment and the employees' assessment is a bit higher (0.177). This correlation is statistically significant, and the higher and more significant correlation with the aggregated measure of employee perceived leadership indicates that aggregation reduces stochastic variation in employee perceptions. The difference between leaders and employees is somewhat smaller for management-by-exception, though the leaders also tend to overrate their leadership behavior relative to the employees. The scores are also lower, 40.1 for the leaders and 32.9 for the employees, resulting in a mean difference of 7.3. Table 3 shows that Pearsons' r correlation between the two is 0.149 (using scores for individual employees) and 0.390 (using aggregated scores). Both correlations are significant at the 0.05 level.

Table 3. Pearson correlations between intended and perceived leadership strategies at individual and organizational level

	Employees as units of analysis	Organizations as units of analysis
Transformational leadership	0.032	0.149
Transactional leadership	0.177*	0.390*
(n)	1,621	79

*$p < 0.05$

Scatterplot showing the associations between the variables on the school level is shown in Figure 2. Summing up, the results show that there are significant differences between the assessments in leadership between employees and leaders, especially for transformational leadership. This supports hypothesis 1. For individual employee scores, the evidence for hypothesis 1b is a bit mixed, given that the association is not significant, while there is no doubt that the concepts (neither for transformational nor for transactional leadership) are so strongly correlated that they can be said to capture the same phenomenon. Given that there is a significant association for transformational leadership when we look at aggregate scores, we conclude that both hypothesis 1a and 1b are supported. We will now see how these different assessments are related to performance and return to a discussion of potential explanations for these differences in the discussion below.

Figure 2. Scatter plots between intended and perceived transactional and transformational leadership strategies (school level, n = 79)

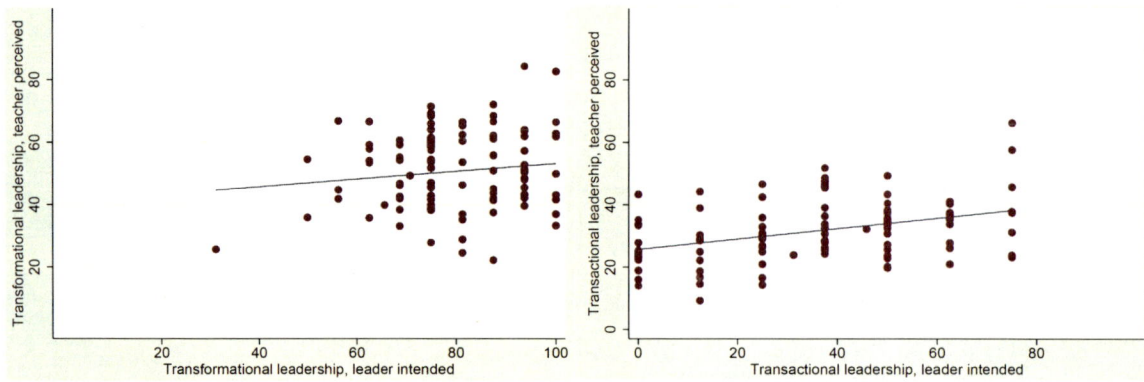

Turning to the relationship between leadership and performance (school effect), Table 4 shows a number of OLS regressions. Model 1 has primarily been included to be able to see how much added explanatory power the leadership variables have. It includes all control variables and shows that leader tenure is positively related with the school effect, but that the leader age is negatively related to the school effect ($p < 0.1$). Concerning differences between the school types, the he school effect is higher at htx. Finally, the school effect may tend to be smaller at big schools (but this association is only borderline significant, $p<0.1$). These associations are almost the same for all the models in Table 4.

Model 2 shows that neither transformational leadership nor management-by-exception as intended by leaders is significantly related to school effects. In contrast, model 3 shows that both leadership strategies as perceived by the employees are closely related to school effects, and this is the case for both types of leadership behavior. The model estimates that the school effect is 0.00637 higher for each point of transformational leadership (on a 0-100 scale) and 0.00778 higher for each point of management-by exception. This result is robust when we include leader's intended leadership strategies as well as employees' perceived leadership strategies (model 4), though the coefficients for employee perceived leadership strategies drop a bit. In sum, the results supports hypothesis 2a and 2b which expect that employee perception of transactional and transformational leadership rather than the leader's intended level of these leadership strategies are positively associated with organizational performance.

We have data available from one externally graded exam (written Danish) from 2012, and to check the robustness of our results, we have run the regressions with this exam as dependent variable (not shown, but available from the authors). Without control for social demographic background, the results are similar and significant, but due to the low number of cases and probably due to the more restricted performance measure (which is ultimately only relevant for teachers in Danish), the results are only borderline significant ($p<0.1$). The coefficients remain more or less the same. This strengthens our belief in the results.

Table 4. OLS regressions of school effects (measured in 2010) by leadership and controls (measured in 2012) (t statistics in parentheses)

	Model 1	Model 2	Model 3	Model 4
Transformational leadership, intended		0.00101		0.000295
		(0.50)		(0.14)
Management-by-exception, intended		-0.000212		-0.000432
		(-0.18)		(-0.40)
Transformational leadership, perceived			0.00637**	0.00487†
			(2.84)	(1.97)
Management-by-exception, perceived			0.00778*	0.00651*
			(2.49)	(2.11)
Teacher age (school mean)	-0.0223	-0.0164	-0.0278	-0.0231
	(-1.36)	(-1.02)	(-1.69)	(-1.38)
Gender composition (share women)	0.0156	-0.0186	0.105	0.0427
	(0.08)	(-0.10)	(0.57)	(0.24)
Tenure in current job (school mean)	0.0148	0.0116	0.0195	0.0162
	(1.11)	(0.90)	(1.45)	(1.25)
Leader age	-0.00904†	-0.0113*	-0.00939†	-0.0114*
	(-1.84)	(-2.38)	(-1.85)	(-2.24)
Leader gender (dummy, female =1)	0.0453	0.0736	-0.0116	0.0258
	(0.63)	(1.01)	(-0.16)	(0.36)
Leader tenure in current position	0.0143***	0.0161***	0.0123**	0.0144***
	(3.70)	(4.38)	(3.28)	(4.06)
School size (# teachers)	-0.00178†	-0.00152	-0.00243*	-0.00199*
	(-1.70)	(-1.55)	(-2.30)	(-2.02)
Stx	0.0282	-0.00119	0.0144	-0.00958
	(0.36)	(-0.02)	(0.20)	(-0.13)
Htx	0.325*	0.255*	0.369**	0.313*
	(2.65)	(2.01)	(3.14)	(2.59)
Hhx (reference)	-	-	-	-
_cons	1.311†	1.118†	1.001	1.023
	(1.90)	(1.65)	(1.53)	(1.55)
N	79	75	79	75
R^2	0.231	0.290	0.321	0.352
adj. R^2	0.131	0.166	0.209	0.214

† $p < 0.1$, * $p < 0.05$, ** $p < 0.01$, *** $p < 0.001$

DISCUSSION AND CONCLUSION

Using data from two surveys, we have investigated the relationship between leaders' assessment of their own leadership strategies and their employees' perceptions of these leadership strategies. The combination with register data has further allowed us to address how these different assessments of leadership relate to organizational performance. Our findings on the first part of the research question show that although leader and employee assessments of leadership are related, the two measures do not seem to capture the same concept. Leaders tend to overrate their use of the leadership strategies relative to their employees' assessment, particularly regarding transformational leadership. The employees' average assessment of the leadership strategies also varies a lot for a given level of leader-reported strategy. The leaders' tendency to overrate their level of transformational leadership could easily be a result of differences in social desirability bias. Employees assess the behavior of another person, while leaders give an assessment of their own behavior, and there are strong expectations concerning the leader role. This may pressure leaders to rate their own level of transformational leadership too high, because they want to live up to standards. The low correlation between the assessments does, however, indicate that there is also a substantial difference between leaders' intended leadership strategy and employees' perceptions of this just as expected by Wright & Nishii (2007). Social desirability bias should primarily increase the level of reported transformational leadership and decrease variation (given that the reported level of transformational leadership comes close to maximum), but there is still a lot a variation in average employee assessments for a given level of leader assessment (as illustrated by figure 2). In sum, it is not plausible that heterogeneous social desirability bias can explain the whole difference between leaders' and employees' assessment of leadership strategy. We therefore suggest that future studies follow the recommendation of Wright and Nishii (2007) and treat the two variables as different concepts.

This recommendation is supported by the results concerning the second part of the research question (about the relationship between organizational performance and leaders'/employees' assessments of leadership). We find that organizational performance is only related to employee perceived leadership strategies and not to the leaders' own answers about their leadership strategies. This suggests that leadership must enter the heads of the employees before it is relevant for organizational consequences. Especially the employees' aggregated assessment of leadership strategies seems to be relevant to include in future studies of leadership and performance.

The relationships between leadership and organizational performance are sizeable and more or less identical in size for transformational and transactional leadership (management-by-exception). This is an indication of the importance of both transactional and transformational leadership practices for performance. In other words, performance is higher, when leaders use either a transactional or a transformational leadership strategy compared to a situation where they use none of the strategies, and the highest performance is observed when both strategies are applied. This leads to a very cautious recommendation of exerting leadership with an iron fist (management-by-exception) but padding it with a velvet glove (transformational leadership).

This recommendation is very cautious due to the limitations of this study in terms of drawing *causal* conclusions. Endogeneity is a very important potential problem, since there may be reverse causality and confounding from unobserved variables associated with both leadership and performance. Leaders may choose their leadership strategy based on earlier performance results, and employees may perceive their leaders as more active, when their organization is performing well. To reduce the last problem, we will switch to performance data from 2013 (exams held after the answers to the two surveys were given) as soon as it is available, but there may still be path dependencies for organizational performance. We therefore strongly recommend that future studies apply experimental designs with random assignments to groups receiving different leadership treatments (see for example Bellé 2013 and Dvir et al. 2002) *and* objective, broad performance indicators, which are determined by longer-term leadership behavior.

For two reasons, this study provides a good stepping stone for future (experimental) research. First, our dependent variable is school effects which are based on objectively measured exam marks adjusted for differences in task difficulty (that is, student socio-economic background). This reduces potential confounding, and school effects are less directly related to the employees' perceptions of how good things are at the school than the actual exam marks. Second, the multilevel structure of the design allows us to compare answers from a given leader with the answers from the employees who are responsible to this specific leader, both individually and aggregating the answers from all relevant employees in the organization. Our findings inform decisions in future studies about measurement of the leadership variables by suggesting that we should always include employee assessments of leadership strategies. Leadership does seem to be in the (aggregated) eye of the employees.

Table A1. Correlation Information

		(1)	(2)	(3)	(4)	(5)	(6)	(7)	(8)	(9)	(10)	(11)	(12)	(13)
(1)	School effect	1.000												
(2)	Transformational leadership (employee)	0.096**	1.000											
(3)	Transactional leadership (employee)	0.227***	-0.476***	1.000										
(4)	Transformational leadership (leader)	0.132***	0.135**	0.119**	1.000									
(5)	Transactional leadership (leader)	0.084*	-0.245***	0.379***	-0.032	1.000								
(6)	Mean teacher age	-0.045	0.030	-0.087*	-0.009	-0.146***	1.000							
(7)	Gender composition (% female)	-0.101**	-0.115***	-0.064*	-0.080*	-0.185***	-0.150***	1.000						
(8)	Mean teacher work experience (current job)	0.043	-0.016	-0.043	-0.069*	-0.130***	0.787***	-0.097***	1.000					
(9)	Leader age	-0.023	-0.048	0.191***	0.113**	0.009	-0.058	0.065	-0.078*	1.000				
(10)	Leader gender	0.050	0.197***	0.138***	0.071*	0.005	-0.142***	-0.136***	-0.098**	-0.029	1.000			
(11)	Leader tenure, current job	0.308***	-0.051	0.177***	0.085*	0.085*	-0.034	-0.054	0.007	0.570***	-0.072*	1.000		
(12)	School size (# teachers)	-0.214***	0.132***	0.105**	0.200***	0.030	-0.028	-0.056	-0.046	0.218***	0.094**	0.073*	1.000	
(13)	Stx	-0.041	0.054	0.142***	0.010	0.005	-0.137***	-0.028	0.043	0.229***	0.110**	0.043	0.317***	1.000
(14)	Htx	0.132**	0.096***	-0.057*	0.181***	0.166***	0.127***	-0.204***	-0.119***	-0.090*	0.084*	-0.026	0.085*	-0.392***

Table A2: Principal axis factoring analyses of latent variables

	Teachers				Principals			
	M	SD	Factor score	Cronbach's alpha	M	SD	Factor score	Cronbach's alpha
Transformational leadership As a leader I.../My principal...	51.79	25.32		0.90	79.35	12.94		0.79
...provide(s) a compelling vision of the organization's future.	3.15	1.11	0.80		4.15	0.65	0.59	
...articulate(s) and generate(s) enthusiasm for a shared vision and mission.	3.03	1.11	0.87		4.22	0.59	0.70	
...facilitate(s) the acceptance of common goals for the school.	2.99	1.07	0.88		4.15	0.68	0.75	
...say(s) things that make employees proud to be part of the organization.	3.12	1.14	0.83		4.21	0.71	0.71	
Management by exception	33.46	22.91		0.51	38.62	23.16		0.63
...focus(es) attention on irregularities, mistakes, exceptions and deviations from what is expected of me.	2.54	1.16	0.49		2.18	1.00	0.56	
...dismiss teachers, if they over a longer period do not perform satisfactory.	2.14	1.07	0.48		2.92	1.16	0.59	

Note: Oblimin rotated

References

Andersen, L. B., & Pallesen, T. (2008). "Not Just for the Money?" How Financial Incentives Affect the Number of Publications at Danish Research Institutions. *International Public Management Journal, 11*(1), 28–47.

Avolio, B. J., Bass, B. M., & Jung, D. I. (1999). Re-examining the components of transformational and transactional leadership using the Multifactor Leadership. *Journal of occupational and organizational psychology, 72*(4), 441–462.

Avolio, B. J., Reichard, R. J., Hannah, S. T., Walumbwa, F. O., & Chan, A. (2009). A meta-analytic review of leadership impact research: Experimental and quasi-experimental studies. *The Leadership Quarterly, 20*(5), 764–784.

Bass, B. M. (1985). *Leadership and performance beyond exceptions.* New York: Free Press.

Bass, Bernard M. (1999). Two decades of research and development in transformational leadership. *European Journal of Work and Organizational Psychology, 8*(1), 9–32.

Bass, Bernard M., & Riggio, R. E. (2006). *Transformational leadership* (2nd ed.). Mahwah, NJ: Lawrence Erlbaum.

Bellé, N. (2013). Leading to Make a Difference: A Field Experiment on the Performance Effects of Transformational Leadership, Perceived Social Impact, and Public Service Motivation. *Journal of Public Administration Research and Theory.* Hentet fra http://jpart.oxfordjournals.org/content/early/2013/06/12/jopart.mut033.short

Burns, J. M. (1978). Leadership. *New Yorker: Harper & Row*.

Dvir, T., Eden, D., Avolio, B. J., & Shamir, B. (2002). Impact of transformational leadership on follower development and performance: A field experiment. *Academy of management journal, 45*(4), 735–744.

Eagly, A. H., & Johnson, B. T. (1990). Gender and leadership style: A meta-analysis. *Psychological bulletin, 108*(2), 233.

Lowe, K. B., Kroeck, K. G., & Sivasubramaniam, N. (1996). Effectiveness correlates of transformational and transactional leadership: A meta-analytic review of the MLQ literature. *The Leadership Quarterly, 7*(3), 385–425.

Meier, K. J., O'Toole, L. J., & Goerdel, H. T. (2006). Management activity and program performance: Gender as management capital. *Public Administration Review, 66*(1), 24–36.

Moynihan, D. P., Pandey, S. K., & Wright, B. E. (2012). Setting the table: How transformational leadership fosters performance information use. *Journal of Public Administration Research and Theory, 22*(1), 143–164.

Nishii, L. H., Lepak, D. P., & Schneider, B. (2008). Employee attributions of the "why" of HR practices: Their effects on employee attitudes and behaviors, and customer satisfaction. *Personnel Psychology, 61*(3), 503–545.

Oberfield, Z. W. (2012). Public Management in Time: A Longitudinal Examination of the Full Range of Leadership Theory. *Journal of Public Administration Research and Theory*. Hentet fra http://jpart.oxfordjournals.org/content/early/2012/12/13/jopart.mus060.short

Park, S. M., & Rainey, H. G. (2008). Leadership and public service motivation in US federal agencies. *International Public Management Journal, 11*(1), 109–142.

Paarlberg, L. E., & Lavigna, B. (2010). Transformational leadership and public service motivation: Driving individual and organizational performance. *Public administration review, 70*(5), 710–718.

Paauwe, J., & Boselie, P. (2005). HRM and performance: what next? *Human Resource Management Journal, 15*(4), 68–83.

Ritz, A. (2009). Public service motivation and organizational performance in Swiss federal government. *International Review of Administrative Sciences, 75*(1), 53–78.

Seltzer, J., & Bass, B. M. (1990). Transformational leadership: Beyond initiation and consideration. *Journal of management, 16*(4), 693–703.

Tekleab, A. G., Sims, H. P., Yun, S., Tesluk, P. E., & Cox, J. (2008). Are we on the same page? Effects of self-awareness of empowering and transformational leadership. *Journal of Leadership & Organizational Studies, 14*(3), 185–201.

Trottier, T., Van Wart, M., & Wang, X. (2008). Examining the nature and significance of leadership in government organizations. *Public Administration Review, 68*(2), 319–333.

Van Knippenberg, D., & Sitkin, S. B. (2013). A Critical Assessment of Charismatic—Transformational Leadership Research: Back to the Drawing Board? *The Academy of Management Annals, 7*(1), 1–60.

Van Wart, M. (2013). Administrative Leadership Theory: A Reassessment After 10 Years. *Public Administration*. Hentet fra http://onlinelibrary.wiley.com/doi/10.1111/padm.12017/full

Wofford, J. C., Whittington, J. L., & Goodwin, V. L. (2001). Follower motive patterns as situational moderators for transformational leadership effectiveness. *Journal of Managerial Issues*, 196–211.

Wright, B. E., Moynihan, D. P., & Pandey, S. K. (2009). Pulling the levers: Leadership, public service motivation and mission valence. I *International Public Service Research Conference, Bloomington, IN*. Hentet fra http://www.indiana.edu/~ipsm2009/Moynihan_Pandey_Wright.pdf

Wright, P. M., & Nishii, L. H. (2007). Strategic HRM and organizational behavior: Integrating multiple levels of analysis. *CAHRS Working Paper Series*, 468.